Obesity and Health

ADAM HIBBERT

W
FRANKLIN WATTS
LONDON·SYDNEY

First published in 2005 by Franklin Watts
96 Leonard Street, London EC2A 4XD

Franklin Watts Australia
45-51 Huntley Street
Alexandria, NSW 2015

Series editor: Rachel Cooke
Series Design: White Design
Picture research: Diana Morris

Dewey Classification: 616.3'98
A CIP catalogue record for this book is available from the British Library.

ISBN: 0 7496 6298 0

Printed in China

Acknowledgements:
Medical data used in this book unless otherwise credited are courtesy of PubMed
(www.ncbi.nlm.nih.gov/entrez), reference numbers: 11337437, 15353530, 15353531, 15494731,
15539977, 15527938, 15494731; Get the Facts Straight, page 5, Social Issues Research Centre, 2005;
Get the Facts Straight, page 9, www.choicesmagazine.org; Facing the Issues, page 11, *Assessment
and Management of Adult Obesity* (the American Medical Association); Facing the Issues, page
17, BBC News; Get the Facts Straight, page 19, *Newsweek*, 20 January 2003.

Photographic credits: Arena/PAL/Topham: 22. Chapman/Topham: 16. David Crausby/Alamy: 12.
Bob Daemmrich/Image Works/Topham: 8. Michael J. Doolittle/Topham: 19.
Gretel Ensignia/National/Topham: 24. Esbin-Anderson /The Image Works/Topham: 18. Mary
Evans PL: 7. Everett Collection/Rex Features: 14. Mauro Fermariello/Science Photo Library: 10.
Brian Harris/Rex Features: front cover, 29. David Hoffman/Alamy: 13. Kevin
Lemarque/Reuters/Corbis: 25t. Richard Lewis/National/Topham: 27. Jeff Morgan/Alamy: 20.
PA/Empics: 15b. PA/Topham: 23, 26bl. Private Collection/Bridgeman Art Library: 6. Rex
Features: 5. Mark Richards/Corbis: 4. Benoit Roland/The Image Works/Topham: 28bl. Scott
Sommerdorf/San Francisco Chronicle/Corbis: 11. Topham: 21, 25b, 26tr. PPA/Topham: 15t.
UT/Corbis: 28tr. Michael S.Yamshita/Corbis: 9. Vinnie Zuffante/Rex Features: 17.
Every attempt has been made to clear copyright. Should there be any inadvertent
omission please apply to the publisher for rectification.

CONTENTS

OBESITY MEANS EXTREME FATNESS.

Bodies come in many shapes and sizes, but if a person is extremely thin or extremely fat this can lead to health problems. The fact that more people – adults and children – are getting fatter is one reason why obesity is hitting the headlines. Another reason is the effect obesity has on the general health, and wealth, of countries.

BODY MASS INDEX

The Body Mass Index (BMI) is a rough guide to healthy weight. Doctors calculate people's BMI by dividing their weight in kilograms by the square of their height in metres ($BMI=kg/m^2$). The result may define whether that person is underweight, healthy, overweight or obese. A healthy BMI score for adults is said to be between 20 and 25. From 25 upwards, there is a greater risk of diabetes, heart attack and other fat-related diseases. A person with a BMI of 30 or above is defined as obese.

Rising obesity rates among children are a cause for concern, although some extreme instances are a result of genetic disorders. This four year old weighs 40 kg.

FAT OR MUSCLE?

The health risks of being overweight are mainly due to fat, which affects the bloodstream, heart and other organs. Some people criticise the BMI because fit, muscular people also score as "overweight". For example, the Australian film star Russell Crowe's weight of 85 kg gives him a BMI of 25. In 2003, US President George W Bush had a BMI of 26.

→ *Actor Russell Crowe's muscles sometimes make him "overweight", according to BMI definitions.*

GET THE FACTS STRAIGHT

Some political debates appear to be based on very little factual evidence – it may become fashionable to focus on a particular social issue, whether or not there are important new reasons for doing so. Obesity may be one such issue. While politicians claim there is an "epedimic" of obesity, the actual UK statistics seem much less dramatic: Between 1995 and 2003, the average weight of 3- to 15-year-old boys fell slightly, from 32kg to 31.9kg. The average for girls between the ages of 3 and 15 rose slightly, from 32kg to 32.4kg. The average 15-year-old boy weighed 60.7kg in 2003, making him 1.9kg heavier than in 1995. The average 15-year-old girl was just 0.4kg heavier in 2003.

OBESE CHILDREN

Many people believe that bad habits learnt in childhood harm a person throughout their life. This is pushing governments around the world to tackle children's fatness, within families and at school. In 2000, American officials took three-year-old Anamarie Martinez-Regino from her parents because she weighed 54 kg, a normal weight for a 15 year old.

EPIDEMIC?

In the 1980s the average weight of the population of many countries began rising. By 2000, countries as different as Japan, the Czech Republic, France and the USA had all recognised that a growing proportion of their population was overweight. But the rise was different in each country – ranging from 5 to 25 per cent – and hard to explain. In particular, changes in calorie intake (see page 9) were not a good predictor of changes in rates of obesity.

MANY WILD ANIMALS *store fat to survive periods without food. But, unlike humans, they use up their store of energy before feeding again. Human beings, our pets and livestock are the only animals to have achieved a secure food supply. This is what allows us to become overweight.*

PREHISTORIC POTBELLIES

Some of the earliest human cultures celebrated fat people. Tiny statues from around 25,000 BC show women with bulky features.

Archaeologists discovered the first of these so-called "Venus figurines" in Willendorf, Austria, in 1908, but they have since found them across Europe and Asia. Their popularity suggests that fat women were highly respected.

ROMANTIC HABITS

Around 2,000 years ago, the Roman Empire created great wealth and luxury for the citizens of Rome. Romans became experts at overeating, indulging in huge feasts. But Romans also valued a body which was fit for war. The Roman writer Seneca recorded, in the 1st century AD, that it was normal to vomit after enjoying a large meal.

⬅ *In the past, feasting was saved for celebrations. As Europe grew wealthier, people could afford to eat more, more often.*

EUROPEAN SCIENCE

Living standards rose in Europe in the 1700s and 1800s, giving more people access to plentiful food. At the same time, medicine was becoming more scientific. In 1835, the Belgian statistician Adolphe Quetelet suggested the Body Mass Index, to help doctors compare the patients they studied. The modern idea of obesity as a health risk dates from this time.

PRIVATE OR PUBLIC?

Statistics such as the BMI make it possible for health to become a public issue, not a private matter between doctor and patient. Since Quetelet, people have argued over whose responsibility health is – the individual's, or society's. In Nazi Germany in the 1930s, good health was made into a duty that each person owed to the state. Some people argue that the Nazi example shows how governments have no business dictating whether someone is healthy or not. Others say that an individual's health has consequences for everyone else (see pages 26–27). Governments react to these changing arguments and attitudes to obesity.

FACING THE ISSUES

Until around 50 years ago, Western European society preferred children to be a bit chubby. According to the popular German nursery tales about Struwwelpeter, "Everybody saw with joy, the plump and hearty, healthy boy" – until he refused his soup and died! In countries where sources of food and medicine are unreliable, chubbiness may still be preferred for children.

⬆ *Struwwelpeter is a collection of cautionary tales, told to children since the 1850s. The story of "Augustus who would not eat his soup" teaches children to think of being "plump" as healthy.*

THE HUMAN BODY *may begin to store energy as fat for a variety of reasons. Most people experience weight gain after periods of heavy eating, for example on traditional feast days such as Christmas. Changes in food supplies may also cause people to put on weight. But for many seriously fat people, weight gain is not simply due to eating too much food.*

➡ *An obese mother and a slightly overweight child may share a gene which causes weight gain. They also share their family's cultural practices and habits.*

IN THE GENES

Children of overweight parents are often overweight themselves. Whether this is mainly due to a similar environment and habits or inherited genes is hard to prove. Studies of adopted children and of twins have not produced clear results. Some serious obesity is caused by genetic abnormalities. But recent changes in the average weight of populations cannot be explained by genes. Changes in diet and lifestyle seem to be the major causes.

SWEET AND FAT

Campaigners against obesity point out two recent additions to the processed foods that are such a large part of many people's diets. The first, introduced in 1971, was fructose, a cheap sugar substitute used in products such as fizzy drinks. Then came palm oil, a vegetable oil that is 45 per cent saturated fat. Both these ingredients improved products' shelf-life and taste, and lowered their prices, but both are also linked to health risks.

GET THE FACTS STRAIGHT – OVERWEIGHT POPULATIONS

Country	Years	Growth in % of overweight individuals	Growth in average daily calorie intake	Average total daily calorie intake
UK	1980–2000	26	220	3312
Australia	1980–1999	23.4	87	3092
USA	1973–2000	16.8	716	3814
Netherlands	1981–2001	11.5	281	3282
Spain	1987–2001	11.1	203	3422
New Zealand	1989–1998	9.1	75	3130
France	1990–2000	6.5	79	3597
Japan	1976–2001	5.8	44	2746
Czech Republic	1993–2001	4.6	69	3097

LIGHT WORK

Calories – units that measure how much energy foods contain – are only stored as fat if this energy is not used up in physical effort. Many studies suggest that, as populations in developed countries have grown fatter, they have actually been eating slightly fewer calories. The point is that people have increasingly inactive lifestyles (see pages 18–19), which means that traditional diets give us too much fuel.

SOCIAL CHANGES

The influence and spread of Western culture has affected the diets and weight levels of people in many parts of the world. On the Pacific island of Kosrae, the arrival of cheap Western food items in the 1980s resulted in huge weight increases – 85 per cent of over-45s became obese. Japan, where once only sumo wrestlers were fat, has also seen rising obesity with the arrival of a more Western diet.

⮕ *Traditional Japanese food rarely leads to obesity. Sumo wrestlers have to eat a special high calorie stew,* **chanko nabe**, *to gain weight.*

ALMOST ALL DOCTORS treat obesity as a serious health risk. Obese people are roughly twice as likely to need hospital treatment than people with BMIs lower than 25. Seriously obese people are more likely to break bones, and their hearts are less able to cope with shocks.

HABITS OR DISEASE?

Doctors advise obese patients to change their eating habits and to improve their fitness through regular exercise. In rare cases (around 1 in 25,000), patients who successfully change their habits find that they stay the same weight. The patient's doctor will then look for diseases that trigger weight gain. These require specialist treatment.

FACING THE ISSUES

Doctors look out for the following problems, among others, when treating obese patients:

- High blood pressure – The bigger a person's body, the harder their heart has to work to pump blood. This can lead to unpleasant conditions, such as varicose veins, and deadly conditions, such as strokes.
- Type II diabetes – In this condition, the body's capacity to process sugars is worn out, leaving harmful levels of sugar in the blood.
- Urinary stress incontinence – Greater body weight can lead to more pressure on the bladder – which in turn causes unintentional urine leakage, for example, when laughing.
- Intertrigo – This condition, which many obese people suffer from, involves chafed and flaky skin, caused by friction and the build-up of moisture within permanent skin creases.
- Osteoarthritis – Extra body weight can wear down cartilage (an elastic tissue) in hip and knee joints and expose the bones to painful rubbing.

← *This doctor is looking out for signs of the special health problems which are associated with obesity as she treats a seriously overweight patient.*

CONTROVERSY

Fat Acceptance campaigners argue that society needs to change its attitudes towards fat people. Many campaigners believe that there is too much emphasis on dieting – which they argue does not result in improved health – and suggest that it is fitness, not fatness, that matters. In May 2000, the US campaigner Marilyn Wann, author of the book *Fat! So?*, won equal rights for fat people in San Francisco. The city's new rules gave Jennifer Portnick, a 110-kg woman, the right to work as a fitness instructor.

Jennifer Portnick (in the blue top) was denied work as a fitness instructor because of her weight, until San Francisco outlawed "fattism".

PUBLIC HEALTH

Doctors' associations offer advice to politicians about health issues. Some of their ideas are about medicines and treatments. Other ideas are less scientific: in May 2004, a spokesman for the British Medical Association was reported as suggesting that fast-food outlets fit narrower doorways to prevent obese customers from entering.

SECOND OPINION

Scientists researching the health effects of obesity have to take into account all aspects of the lives of fat people and thin people. This way they can check that it is obesity, and not something else, which is responsible for any differences they notice between the health of the two groups. Some diseases are now firmly associated with obesity (see box).

EVERY SOCIETY HAS ITS OWN notions about the ideal human body. Society also affects our bodies by deciding what foods there are to choose from. Food producers use advertising to persuade customers to eat their products. Other groups press for governments to police food quality, or argue against consuming too much.

FAT IS A FIJIAN ISSUE

The *jubu vina*, or "well-formed", Fijian is traditionally much heavier than the Western ideal. Successful people on the Pacific islands of Fiji, including royalty, are expected to eat well and to have powerful, well-fuelled bodies. But with the arrival of television in 1995, styles are changing. Fijian girls are now more likely to diet.

RELIGIOUS RULES

Christianity, among other religions, warns that physical pleasures can make us selfish. According to this religious point of view, eating for pleasure, rather than need, weakens our ability to be useful to our fellow humans. In 2003, French chef Paul Bocuse launched a campaign to ask the Catholic Church to remove *gourmandise* (gluttony) from its list of deadly sins.

← These Fijian women conform to traditional Fijian ideas of beauty; being large is a sign of strength. A skinny woman is seen as weak and unfit.

AGAINST CONSUMERS

Even non-religious people find greediness unattractive. Some organise campaigns to argue that selfish consumption causes inequality or harms the environment. In September 2004, the Canadian environmental campaigning group Adbusters went to court to win the right to put its adverts on TV – adverts that showed Western consumers as selfish pigs, brainwashed by advertising.

FATTISM?

The International Size Acceptance Association (ISAA) argues that anyone who says that fat people are greedy, lazy, weak or stupid is guilty of fattism – an offence, according to the ISAA, as great as racism or sexism. The ISAA, based in Texas, USA, defines fattism, or size discrimination, as "any action which places people at a disadvantage simply because of their size".

"Junk" food such as fried potato chips is cheap and filling, often as a result of its salt and fat content. Some argue that food advertising makes people more greedy.

WHAT DO YOU THINK?

We value our friends' advice to help us avoid making bad choices. But...

- Do you have the right to assume that a friend's overweight size is due to bad choices?
- Should you tell a friend who, in your opinion, appears fat that they should exercise more?
- Does telling someone they are fat help them to manage their weight, or does it just undermine their confidence?

SOCIAL PRESSURES ACT on children and adults. Different people respond to these pressures in different ways. Parents' efforts to prevent their children from becoming overweight can be effective, but they can also backfire – causing children to have guilty feelings about their bodies. And feelings that develop in childhood often remain when a person becomes an adult.

THE PERFECT BODY

Studies in Germany show that men and women with the eating disorders anorexia and bulimia have the same notions about the "ideal body" as others. But their idea of their own body is false – they see themselves as fatter than they are. Larger people, in contrast, may not accept the standard view of the ideal body. Their size does not feel less than ideal – it is just what suits their way of life.

REBELLION

Larger people can also react against being forced to look or behave in a certain way. Being heavy, some argue, is one way to show independence from peer pressure. It can also make a person harder to push around. In the 1990s, the American rap stars Big Pun and the Notorious B.I.G. brought this idea of power through size to mainstream culture.

↙ The Notorious B.I.G., born Christopher Wallace, was a Brooklyn rap artist whose severe obesity (BMI: 47) was a badge of independence and defiance.

CONTROL

Other people respond to emotional difficulty by eating less. As a child, the catwalk model Sophie Dahl began to refuse food to prove she had some control over her own life. Her family had suddenly moved from a place where she had been happy and had had many friends. Changing her eating habits was a reaction to being powerless to decide where her family lived.

← Sophie Dahl grew up to become a "plus-size" fashion model, before choosing a slimmer figure.

FACING THE ISSUES

Laura Rhodes, a 13-year-old schoolgirl from Wales, committed suicide in 2003. She claimed she had been bullied about her weight, although her school denied this. However, before her death, she wrote of her feelings of low self-esteem:

"I was a shocking size 24, I just ate and ate, I didn't care anymore, I shoved myself into [my uniform] and went down stairs. I put in my lunch box and I felt my heart start to beat faster, and gripping pain inside myself, but no, this wasn't a special day, this was every day. This had gone on for a few weeks now, I was fat, ugly and worthless."

← Laura Rhodes shortly before her death.

COMFORT FOOD

There is often a relationship between the amount of food a person eats and his or her mental well-being. Some people eat food for comfort when they are sad or nervous. This may occur more for people who lack the power to change their circumstances or overcome the sources of their anxiety. This seems a very basic instinct. It has been noted that stress and poor health increase near the bottom of the social hierarchy in groups of primates, such as chimpanzees.

IN SOME PARTS OF THE WORLD,

low weight is still a major health problem. But for a growing section of the world's population, eating too much is becoming a bigger health risk. China and India, two developing countries with a combined population of 2.4 billion people, are both suffering from increases in obesity-related illnesses such as diabetes.

Wealthy countries require food producers to list ingredients on each packet, so that consumers can make informed choices.

CHOOSING FOOD

Adults, unlike children, can choose the food they buy, though wealthy people will always have a wider choice than poor people. In Australia in May 2004, McDonalds introduced nutrition labels on its packaging to help consumers work out what to choose. Other countries are looking at ways to demand this labelling on all fast food.

CUTTING CALORIES

Many adults try to lose weight by going on diets that reduce their calorie intake. This can have dramatic effects over a short period. But research suggests that most people regain weight after sudden dieting. The pattern of dieting and putting weight back on is described as "yo-yoing", and may be harmful to physical and mental health. A few people resort to the risky but effective route of stomach surgery.

➜ *TV celebrity Roseanne Barr had her stomach made smaller by a surgeon to help control her weight.*

FACING THE ISSUES

In countries with major HIV/Aids epidemics, attitudes towards size are often turned on their head. Zimbabwean Thoko Elphick-Pooley explains:

"In a country like Zimbabwe, where an estimated 1.4m people are suspected to be living with HIV/Aids, you just cannot contemplate losing weight without fearing that your neighbours will start whispering that you have Aids. Men and women alike feel comfortable dating a fat, big person because they are considered 'clean'. Hence one colloquial name for Aids in Africa is 'slim'."

BURNING CALORIES

Physical exercise is usually a good route to health. Whether or not exercise lowers weight, a fit person is less likely to develop breathing, blood circulation or heart problems. Brisk walking is one way to get fit. In 2004, a UK manufacturer of potato crisps offered free pedometers to help people check if they were reaching a target of 10,000 steps per day. Over a million people ordered one.

NO WORRIES

Many adults do not worry about their weight. On average, people tend to eat more and drink more alcohol when they settle down with a partner – so weight may be a sign of being content. By some definitions, health is whatever suits your goals. Choosing to enjoy our food without worrying about the consequences might add to our quality of life, even if it reduces the "quantity" of life we have.

Children enjoy strong flavours, such as in salty, sweet and fatty foods.

CHILDREN'S WEIGHT IS measured using different criteria to adults, since it is normal for children to have plenty of fat to power growth spurts. Instead of using the Body Mass Index (see pages 4 and 5), doctors assess children as overweight if they score in the top 5 per cent for their age group, and underweight if they are in the bottom 5 per cent.

FAMILY HABITS

Since the mid-20th century, one major social change that has affected many countries has been the rise of working mothers. In 1900, 5 per cent of mothers worked. By 2000, that number was close to 65 per cent. With less time to prepare meals, families rely more on processed, factory food. Children eat less fresh food and more snacks, instead of sitting down to a structured, family meal.

FOOD FEATURES

Television can have an influence on the foods that children favour. Only larger food producers can afford to buy TV advertising. Their products often contain more of the fats and sugars that lead to obesity. So children are taught to prefer foods that may be bad for them. In February 2004, the US health research organisation the Kaiser Family Foundation found that watching TV did not make children lazier, but that "junk food" adverts affected their preferences.

APRON STRINGS

Parents today are less confident of their children's safety in public than ever before. They have lost trust in other adults, even though risks to children have generally decreased. Parents – particularly in poor neighbourhoods – may prefer their children to be indoors where they are "safe", even if they miss out on energetic games with friends. Limits on children's outdoor activities, together with the long hours many spend watching TV and playing computer games, can contribute to obesity.

CAR CULTURE?

Some people believe that children who could exercise by walking or cycling to school should not be driven in cars by their parents. But research published in the British Medical Journal in 2004 rejects this idea. According to the research, walking or cycling to school accounts for just 2 per cent of a child's weekly exercise. According to this research, sports or physical play, such as skateboarding, is far more important.

GET THE FACTS STRAIGHT

Bottom heavy? According to this 2002 league table, children in southern European countries are fatter than children in more northerly ones.

Country	% of overweight 10-year-olds
Italy	36
Greece	31
Spain	30
USA	25
Britain	22
France	17
Australia	16
Germany	15
Netherlands	14

⬇ Most children enjoy some physical play, which helps growing bodies and burns calories.

⬆ *School dinners which are both healthy and appealing to children are becoming more available.*

THERE ARE MANY SOLUTIONS

available for people who are worried about overweight children. Politicians and health experts have to find a balance between preventing children from eating poor foods and providing more opportunities for them to take exercise. Education is the easiest part of children's lives to change, but some countries also hope to influence children's choices as consumers.

SCHOOL DIET

Many countries around the world are taking action to change the types of food served at school. In Italy, France, Denmark, Sweden, Austria and Germany, new rules set by governments are making schools serve their pupils organic foods. In the USA, however, efforts to change school food have been delayed by the concerns of existing food suppliers, who need the "school food programme" to buy their surplus produce.

TEACHING PRIORITIES

School children in France and Germany devote twice as much time to sports lessons than British children. Many British schools have sold playing fields in recent years to earn cash to pay for other areas of teaching. These changes are one reason why British children are fatter than their French or German counterparts.

TEACHING HEALTHY LIFESTYLES

In July 2004, the Australian federal government invited schools and parents' groups to apply for grants to help fight obesity. Health minister Tony Abbott offered up to $1,500 to each organisation, to support projects such as healthier canteen menus, school vegetable gardens and healthy cooking classes.

CONTROLLING ATTITUDES

Some critics of "junk food" believe that children need to be protected from advertising, which manipulates their feelings about food. Sweden has banned advertising to children on Swedish-based TV since 1991, including food adverts. While it is still unclear whether this ban has reduced Swedish children's intake of junk food, campaigners in Europe, Australia and the USA want to copy Sweden's example.

⊕ *Schools with the time and resources for plenty of sport help pupils stay fit and alert.*

FACING THE ISSUES

In 1999, Leeds Metropolitan University in the UK established the Carnegie International Weight Loss Camp, which children between the ages of 11 and 17 can attend during school holidays to lose weight, adopt a healthier lifestyle and make new friends. One of the first young people to attend the so-called "Fat camp" reported: "I could talk to people there and they understood because they'd been through it too. It was lots of fun and we had a real laugh. I tried all sorts of activities and I now go to the gym, circuit train at least twice a week and I exercise at home in the morning and before I go to bed. I also play basketball at school."

TWO OPPOSING THEMES about obesity compete for space in the media. On the one hand, people very often discuss obesity in terms of it being a medical complaint. On the other hand, we sometimes hear that it is good to resist peer pressure, and that being different by being big is okay.

➲ *Deborah Voigt is one of many opera stars whose larger bodies add power to their singing voice.*

SHOCK! HORROR!

Media stories about everyday events can seem boring – so many television, newspaper and Internet reports tend to focus on dramatic or shocking stories. If someone loses a few kilograms on a gentle weight-loss programme, it is not news. If a fat celebrity such as the US actress Roseanne Barr (see page 17) loses 33 kg – the weight of a 10-year-old boy – after stomach surgery, that is news! There are countless examples of celebrities featuring in the press because of their weight problems.

PUBLIC OPINION?

Fat Acceptance campaigners, as well as feminists, often accuse the media of promoting slim figures. Media owners respond that they are simply giving the public what it wants. But this desire can affect the quality of some art forms. In 2004, the Royal Opera House in London cancelled Deborah Voigt's role as Ariadne in the opera *Ariadne auf Naxos.* Even though Voigt is regarded as having the best voice in the world for the part, the director wanted a slimmer singer.

COMMERCIAL RULES

Most media are funded by advertisements. Food producers are some of the biggest advertisers. So media publishers might be careful to limit stories criticising their clients. But food producers' messages are not always predictable. In France in 2002, McDonalds adverts told mothers not to feed their children more than one McDonalds meal per week.

SELLING THE TRUTH

Officials have to stop advertisers lying to consumers. Radio adverts told American consumers that a new diet supplement, Body Solutions, would make them lose weight while they slept. In 2003, government investigators took the company to court and forced it to close down, but not before it had earned an estimated $150 million from gullible customers.

GET THE FACTS STRAIGHT

A great many female models and actresses are moderately or severely underweight. On top of their extreme low weight, photos and films are now digitally altered to make them appear even thinner. This list of famous women divides their weight into three BMI categories: low normal, underweight and severely underweight.

● BMIs low normal

Courtney Love	62.7 kg (138 lbs)
Kate Winslet	59 kg (130 lbs)
Laetitia Casta	57.3 kg (126 lbs)
Drew Barrymore	53.6 kg (118 lbs)
Madonna	52.3 kg (115 lbs)

● BMIs underweight

Ashley Judd	56.8 kg (125 lbs)
Anna Kournikova	55.9 kg (123 lbs)
Angelina Jolie	54.5 kg (120 lbs)
Helen Hunt	55 kg (121 lbs)
Lisa Kudrow	53.6 kg (118 lbs)
Portia De Rossi	53.2 kg (117 lbs)
Milla Jovovich	52.7 kg (116 lbs)

● BMIs severely underweight

Kirsten Dunst	48.2 kg (106 lbs)
Courtney Cox	45.5 kg (100 lbs)

Images of "superwaif" models in the media make larger women seem unusual.

IF OBESITY CAUSES POOR HEALTH

it is bad news for employers, who will lose earnings when their workers take sick leave. But public health efforts to tackle obesity might also harm food retailers' businesses. These retailers form lobby groups to advise politicians, and to present the food industry's side of the argument to the public.

⊙ Fear of being overweight is good for business in industries like this one which sell "slimming" services and treatments.

THE CUSTOMER IS KING

If consumers demand sweet drinks, businesses will sell those products. Changes in consumer choices affect what producers make. Between 2002 and 2003, sugared soft drinks lost 1.5 per cent market share to low-calorie soft drinks. Coca Cola and Pepsi both responded to the change in 2004 with new low-calorie options.

OBESITY – THE CONSUMER'S CHOICE

Food producers emphasise the importance of consumer responsibility for obesity. In 1961, Frank R Neu, an American dairy industry spokesman, warned, "We may be sitting ourselves to death". In 2004, the US Congress passed the Personal Responsibility in Food Consumption Act, to protect retailers from being sued by overweight customers.

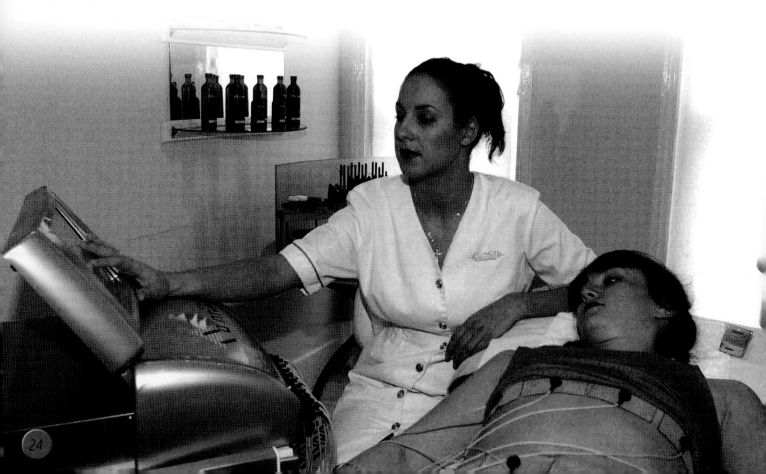

THE FOREVER DIET

The "diet industry" sells products such as books, low-calorie foods, courses, electronic gadgets, and supplements meant to limit the appetite. Globally, it earns over $50 billion per year from people hoping to lose weight. Some argue that the industry encourages people to feel ashamed of their weight to win new customers.

DRUG BARONS?

Drugs companies stand to make good profits from medicines that help treat obesity. The manufacturers point out that some of the profits they make from such drugs pay for research into the causes and risks of obesity. One prescription weight-loss drug is "Meridia", produced by the US firm Abbott Laboratories. If it is not properly administered, it can cause heart problems. Patients accept the possible side effects of the drug to avoid the health risks of obesity.

⬆ *Dr David J Graham, of the US Food and Drug Administration (FDA), has highlighted the dangers of "Meridia" if not properly administered.*

FACING THE ISSUES

In 2004, a New York film-maker called Morgan Spurlock released *Super Size Me*, a film documenting what happened to him when he decided to eat nothing but fast food for a month. A shocking decline in health, weird cravings for greasy food, and an unhappy girlfriend are the results. The film raised so much controversy that many fast-food chains ended the practice of "supersizing" meals – upgrading drinks, burgers and fries to the largest size for a small extra cost.

⬆ *Spurlock's "reality TV" treatment of the fast food business caught the public's attention and led businesses to change their menus.*

GOVERNMENTS *that provide health care for their citizens usually try to prevent the cost of this care from rising. One solution is to stop people becoming ill. So governments try to change consumer behaviour in as many ways as possible, such as through education, advertising and taxation.*

GAIN WITHOUT PAIN?

Tackling consumer habits is a low-cost option for acting against obesity. In November 2004, the UK government suggested new laws to change consumer behaviour. But critics pointed out that the government was doing little about issues that would cost much more to fix – such as poverty and bad housing. These issues can sometimes be linked to obesity.

⬆ *Efforts to change consumer attitudes to smoking are working, but can have unforeseen consequences.*

USING OUTRAGE

In 2004, a committee of British politicians released a report about obesity that highlighted the death of a three-year-old obese girl. The report led to public outrage against the unknown parents. The girl's death was later revealed to be due to a genetic disorder – but the politicians won national and international attention for their focus on obesity. Just like anti-smoking and AIDs awareness campaigns, shock tactics can be effective.

⬅ *In 2004, UK Health Minister, John Reid, proposed laws to make "healthy choices" clear to consumers. He used some "shock tactics" to make his point.*

SIDE EFFECTS?

Public health campaigns can have unexpected effects. Obesity may have risen partly as a result of the success of anti-smoking campaigns. Ex-smokers eat more and run a greater chance of becoming overweight. Health campaigns can have unexpected costs, too. Early deaths among risk-takers (be they smokers or unhealthy eaters) save taxpayers the cost of their pensions and nursing care. But obesity can also be very expensive, in terms of health care costs and lost working days.

FIGHTING FLAB

Obesity even has implications for national security. In Italy in 2004, a volunteer soldier, referred to in the media as "Francesca", sued the Italian army after it sacked her for being too fat to perform her military duties. Many countries have recorded rising levels of unfitness in volunteers for their armed forces.

WHAT DO YOU THINK?

- Do you think it is fair that taxpayers should pay for the health care costs of risk-taking individuals, such as those who smoke heavily, or eat and drink in large amounts?
- Do you think governments should use shock tactics to try to warn people of the risks of obesity?
- Do you think changing consumer behaviour is the best way for governments to tackle obesity?

Good public health cuts health care costs, but as more people survive into old age, pension costs grow.

FAT FUTURES

OBESITY IS NO LONGER *treated as a personal health problem. Governments are likely to take more responsibility for controlling our weight. They can intervene in several ways, such as censorship, controls on food production and special taxes. But changes in science and culture might also affect our weight.*

⊕ *In the future, scientists may find a way of making ice-cream and other "junk foods" a healthy choice.*

⊕ *John Banzhaf, the US legal expert behind lawsuits against tobacco businesses, has turned his attention to fighting obesity.*

HEALTH CARE PRICING

Some health care systems are beginning to treat "self-inflicted" harms differently to other health problems. Smokers, for example, are expected to pay more for their health insurance. In September 2004, US activist John Banzhaf successfully asked the US government to allow insurance companies to charge obese persons more for their health coverage.

FUTURE FOOD

Food science also offers the possibility of preventing obesity. Olestra is a type of fat, first discovered in 1968, which passes undigested through the body, making it very low in calories. Problems with diarrhoea, however, mean that it is still not widely used – although scientists are working to overcome this. Another scientific discovery is adenosine monophosphate, or AMP, produced by the US biotechnology firm Linguagen and approved by food officials in September 2004. AMP blocks bitterness in food, making it taste sweeter without adding sugar.

FOOD CONTROLS

Governments are likely to make it harder for new materials – for example, genetically-modified (GM) crops – to be used by food producers. This might delay the introduction of new, tasty, low-calorie foods. At the same time, governments may introduce taxes on fat and sugar, to force producers to use less of them. Without the attraction of sweet, fatty food, people may choose to eat less anyway.

HISTORIC TREND?

It may be that the world's population is at the beginning of a weight "transition", after which more of us will always be overweight. Yet life expectancy – the number of years the average person can expect to live – continues to improve in most countries. We may find that we simply learn to live with our rounder figures.

WHAT DO YOU THINK?

Technology might allow us to solve some obesity problems without changing people's habits, but...

- Should money be invested to replace fattening foods with new ingredients?
- If genetically-modified foods could be created to prevent obesity, would you oppose or support the research?
- Do you think it is up to the individual to control his or her own weight, without such help?

The shape of things to come? As people's shapes change, so will cultural attitudes.

GLOSSARY

anorexia: Health-threatening eating disorder in which a person's appetite fails or is ignored so he or she becomes dangerously underweight.

biotechnology: Technology which uses or adapts the functions of biological materials.

bulimia: Eating disorder in which "binge" eating is followed by efforts to purge the body, for example by vomiting.

censorship: Limiting the public's access to certain types of information.

consumer responsibility: Respecting consumers' ability to take decisions.

developed country: Country with an urban economy based around high technology.

developing country: Country with a farming economy based around low technology but where there is a shift towards the cities and industries.

diabetes: Inability of the body to process sugars, causing a variety of health risks.

epidemic: Outbreak of disease, normally used to describe the spread of a virus.

fattism: Belief that people's capacities and rights differ according to their weight.

feminist: Political activist opposed to sexism, promoting women's rights.

genes: The instructions for building an organism found in the DNA of each cell.

genetically-modified (GM) food: Food produced from plants or animals containing artificial genes.

health care: Services provided by doctors, nurses and other health professionals.

heart attack: Failure of the heart to pump blood, a major cause of death.

HIV/Aids: Blood-borne viral disease that attacks the body's immune system so it cannot fight disease. Without drug treatments, it is fatal.

junk food: Slang for cheap, processed food, high in calories but low in nutrients.

market share: Percentage of an industry's customers that choose one company's goods.

Nazi: Political party in Germany in the 1930s and 1940s led by the dictator, Adolf Hitler.

organic food: Food produced without the use of artificial chemicals, fertilisers or drugs.

pedometer: Pocketable device which records the number of steps the bearer has taken.

peer pressure: Approval, scorn and other opinions of your friends or classmates – your "peers" or equals.

racism: Belief that people's capacities and rights differ according to their skin colour or ethnic origin.

saturated fat: Usually solid at room temperature, a fat found in meat and dairy products, as well as some vegetable oils. It raises blood cholesterol, which increases the risk of heart attack.

sexism: Belief that people's capacities and rights differ according to their sex.

social hierarchy: Any set of relationships in which some people (or animals) have more power than others.

stomach surgery: Removing or tying-off a part of the stomach, so helping the patient eat less.

stroke: When blood bursts through an artery wall into the brain, causing brain damage.

The websites listed here will help you look further into obesity and the issues surrounding it. Many of these sites have links to other sites.

UK

www.toast-uk.org.uk
The Obesity Awareness and Solutions Trust. A charity that encourages a better understanding of obesity.

www.bbc.co.uk/science/ hottopics/obesity/index.shtml
Information from the British Broadcasting Corporation's (BBC) website about obesity, with links to other sites.

www.nationalobesityforum. org.uk
The National Obesity Forum.

www.dietproject.org.uk
The website of the Scottish Community Diet Project, which aims to improve Scotland's diet and health.

www.foodfitness.org.uk
A UK food industry-sponsored site promoting advice on healthy eating.

AROUND THE WORLD

www.healthinsite.gov.au
Up-to-date information on important health topics, including obesity.

www.asso.org.au
Australasian Society for the Study of Obesity.

www.coolfoodplanet.org
Food information site for children, from the European Food Information Council.

www.easoobesity.org
European Association for the Study of Obesity.

www.childhoodobesity.net
European Childhood Obesity Group – a research organisaton.

www.iotf.org
International Obesity Task Force – International Association for the Study of Obesity.

www.bigfatblog.com
Big Fat Blog links to and gives opinions on articles dealing with fat, aiming to offer up a fat-positive opinion.

http://showmethedata.info/
Fact-busting for fat acceptors.

www.size-acceptance.org
International Size Acceptance Association (ISAA).

www.consumerfreedom.com
Industry-backed campaign to prevent controls on catering and food retailing.

FURTHER READING

Fat Land: How Americans Became the Fattest People in the World
Greg Critser, Penguin Books
An ex-fattie explores the complex causes of the growth in overweight people in modern America.

The Obesity Myth: Why America's Obsession with Weight Is Hazardous to Your Health
Paul Campos, Gotham Books
A law professor raises doubts about the value of anti-obesity policies and the diet industry.

The Hungry Gene
Ellen Ruppel Shell, Atlantic Books
A science journalist explores the best scientific research into the causes of obesity.

The Atlas of Food: Who Eats What, Where and Why
Millstone & Lang, Earthscan
An interesting, well-illustrated tour of the world's varied eating habits and food items.

It's Your Health: Eating Properly; Exercise; Self-esteem
Three titles in a series published by Franklin Watts which give information and practical advice on how to develop a more healthy lifestyle.

INDEX